Y0-AGT-987

MONSTER TRUCKS & TRACTORS

COLONIAL BEACH SCHOOL LIBRARY
COLONIAL BEACH, VIRGINIA

RACE CAR LEGENDS

COLLECTOR'S EDITION

Jeff Burton

Dale Earnhardt Jr.

Famous Finishes

Famous Tracks

Kenny Irwin Jr.

Jimmie Johnson

The Labonte Brothers

Lowriders

Monster Trucks & Tractors

Motorcycles

Off-Road Racing

Rockcrawling

Tony Stewart

The Unsers

Rusty Wallace

MONSTER TRUCKS
& TRACTORS

Sue Mead

CHELSEA HOUSE
PUBLISHERS

Cover Photo: *Monster Patrol* drives over two cars at Lowe's Motor Speedway in Concord, North Carolina.

CHELSEA HOUSE PUBLISHERS

VP, New Product Development   Sally Cheney
Director of Production   Kim Shinners
Creative Manager   Takeshi Takahashi
Manufacturing Manager   Diann Grasse

STAFF FOR MONSTER TRUCKS & TRACTORS

Editorial Assistant Sarah Sharpless
Production Editor Bonnie Cohen
Photo Editor Pat Holl
Series Design and Layout Hierophant Publishing Services/EON PreMedia

Original edition first published in 1999.
© 2006 by Chelsea House Publishers.

http://www.chelseahouse.com

First Printing

1   3   5   7   9   8   6   4   2

Library of Congress Cataloging-in-Publication Data

Mead, Sue.
   Monster trucks & tractors/Sue Mead.
      p. cm.—(Race car legends. Collector's edition)
   Includes bibliographical references and index.
   ISBN 0-7910-8689-5
   1. Monster trucks—Juvenile literature. 2. Truck racing—Juvenile literature.
3. Monster trucks—History—Juvenile literature. 4. Truck racing—Juvenile literature.
5. Farm tractors—History—Juvenile literature. 6. Tractor driving—Competitions—
Juvenile literature. I. Title: Monster trucks and tractors. II. Title. III. Series.
TL230.15.M43 2005
796.7–dc22

                                                                2005011370

TABLE OF CONTENTS

THE MONSTERS: BOB AND DAN AND THE MONSTER TRUCKS

Some would say that monster trucks are some of the wildest and whackiest beasts on the planet. But you probably wouldn't hear Bob Chandler say that because he's the guy who started the whole craze.

Bob loved to tinker with cars. It all started during his teenage years when he took cars apart and put them back together again. He'd take "old junk and make 'em into street vehicles and hotrods, doing things like putting in three carburetors." He drove a pickup truck to high school and was an outcast because "it was *before* trucks were popular."

After military service and time in college, Bob and his family took a three-month trip to Alaska. While driving along the rigorous **Alcan highway**, Bob says, "the highway tore the tires of our **four-wheel-drive (4WD)** camper to shreds and someone in Alaska gave me some bigger and tougher tires for the trip home."

Home was in St. Louis, Missouri, where Bob had a construction job and drove a Ford F-250 4 × 4 for work and play. When he needed parts for his truck, there was no place close

Bob Chandler's famous monster truck, *Bigfoot*, started the monster truck craze.

to buy them or get repair work done, so in 1974, he opened up a 4WD shop, The Midwest Four-Wheel Drive Center. For Bob, "it was the right time and the right place." He says that he never had an idea ahead of his time, but because of his experience on the Alcan highway, he had a concept of "bigger could be better," so he added bigger tires, engines, and axles to keep ahead of everybody else in the **4 × 4** business.

Parts at his shop sold like hot cakes as he modified his trucks and started competitions such as hill climbs. He soon realized that beating his customers wasn't smart so he moved out of competition and into exhibition. As his trucks became "bigger and better" *Bigfoot* was born. The name came from Bob's shop manager who called Bob "Bigfoot" because he couldn't keep his foot off the throttle, and sometimes broke parts on his truck. Soon, the new design wore the name.

In his first shows with *Bigfoot*, he used 48-inch tires on a Ford F-250 pickup truck. After he established a reputation with *Bigfoot*, competitors *King Kong* and *USA #1* came along, and Bob decided to go bigger again. *Bigfoot II* hit the arena with 66-inch tires, and overnight, the truck's now-famous name became a household word.

In 1981, Bob started his next adventure: car crushing. He began by driving over two cars in a farm field for fun. Soon, this new trick caught the eye of promoters and created a craze that has skyrocketed in popularity.

Today, Bob and his fleet of Bigfoots have been to 17 countries. Most of the monster trucks are in Stage One of monster truck development, or the 10,000- to 12,000-pound range. Bob has built muscle-bound 4 × 4s as heavy as 20,000 pounds. Now, Bob Chandler Jr. has taken over Bigfoot 4 × 4, and he and his father are working on Stage Three trucks that have lighter fiberglass bodies, a tubular chassis, and up to 30 inches of suspension travel. They are experimenting with a straight-axle truck and with independent suspension in the front and rear, so all the tires will work independently. This will provide better handling and a better ride and improved cornering capability.[1]

The competition field has evolved into pairs, or side-by-side racing, and features trucks with 575-cubic-inch supercharged engines and other styles of competition. These machines can produce more than 2,000 horsepower and can hit 80 miles per hour (mph). Bigfoot 4 × 4 has an impressive fleet of monster trucks (six racing trucks, three display trucks, two speciality trucks, and seven alumni trucks), video games, a website, and a huge international fan club. "There's little money in racing," says Bob, Jr. "when the trucks cost between $150,000 and $250,000 each, need engine work

The monster truck, *Snake Bite*, crushes a row of cars under its tires in side-by-side competition with another monster.

after every race, and burn two to three gallons of methanol racing fuel in a 250-ft. run."

For Dan Patrick, racing tractors and trucks is just about as American as apple pie. He doesn't remember a time when the guys in his family weren't putting a horse, tractor, or truck on the line for a wager. "It's part of our family's history since the 1920s," he says. "A matter of who had the best horse or the best tractor."

Dan grew up on a livestock and grain farm in Kingston, Ohio, and worked with his dad 365 days a year. He realized how hard the work on a farm was and what little financial reward was in store. "When I was a child, it was natural to just pull things on the farm, and then on the weekends go to the tractor pulls."

Dan started pulling in 1972 when he was 17 and competed at the local and state levels. In 1983, he traveled across the United States and Canada to pulling competitions and he was placed seventh overall in the **Modified Class**. He became tired of adding and taking off weights to make the same tractor bump up in weight from 5,000 to 12,000 pounds for different events and became interested in truck pulling instead.

In 1985, when tractor and truck pulls became popular and promoters asked competitors to enter, Dan was asked to build a "funny car." *Warlord* became Dan's transition into monster trucks. Over the next four years, he built two funny cars, and in 1987, he built and introduced the first dragster puller.

Dan broadened his operations in 1988 and bought *Samson*, which joined the United Sports of America's Motor Spectacular as a competitor. Six months later, he was hired by Bob Chandler to build the next generation of trucks for Bob's Bigfoot fleet. During his three years with this crew as a designer and driver, Dan was instrumental in developing and changing the industry. When he saw the need for unique trucks, each with its own personality and character, Dan decided to open his own business.

"What I do today is build the chassis for others, build component parts, and act as a consultant. In one year, I've raced 40 events and built five trucks. I enjoy all aspects, but I love building the most. I want somebody to say with pride that they have a Dan Patrick truck." Involved in motorsports for over 30 years, Dan has won numerous awards, including Truck of the Year, Wreck of the Year, a sportsmanship award, a Safety Award and the Innovative Award from the U.S. Hot Rod Association (USHRA). Once Safety and Rules Director for the Monster Truck Racing Association (MTRA), he is now the world's largest manufacturer of monster trucks.[2]

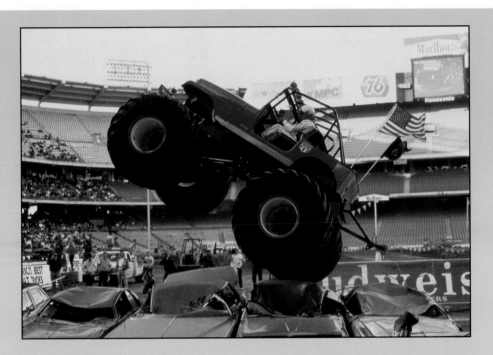

The roll bars, shown here on *Hot Stuff*, ensure a degree of safety for monster truck drivers.

Carl and the Monster Tractors

Carl Fowler grew up on a dairy farm in Pownal, Vermont. That meant he had to milk cows: every morning and night, every day of the week, every week of the year. He hated to milk cows but he loved tractors and today he lives, eats, and breathes these monster machines.

When Carl graduated from high school, he went to work for a tractor dealer and soon he became a dealer himself. He began to collect tractors. He collected mostly antique models; at one time, he had dozens of them. That meant he had to build barns to store them. "It's like a disease," he says, "once you get started, it's hard to stop."

Before long, Carl got hooked on tractor competitions called tractor pulls. Over the years, he has pulled almost every type of tractor there is. Carl will tell you, that's where the real fun begins. When he talks about competing, his 54-year-old face lights up and his eyes sparkle. He will pull out two of the trade magazines, *Tractor Puller* and *The Hook*, and begin to tell you stories of his experiences.

Carl started to compete in the **Antique Class** where classic models (built before 1960) pull loads of up to 32,000 pounds on a stone or wooden boat. He worked his way up to

DID YOU KNOW?

Bigfoot performs at over 900 events a year, including birthday parties that are Bigfoot-themed, with a children's play area that has remote-controlled vehicles and drivable kid's cars. *Bigfoot* has expanded its mail order and Internet sales and sells toys, T-shirts, pictures, and over 50 other items, including go-karts. Sales have quintupled over the past five years. The company is currently exploring the possibility of a drivable Bigfoot truck for kids.*

Since 1992, Dan has built 70 monster trucks. His original truck, *Warlord*, is in Orlando, Florida, at the Race Rock Cafe on permanent display and his muscle truck, *Samson*, created as a 3-D design in 1993 for the television show *American Gladiators*, has performed across the country and gained popularity with each performance.**

Modified tractors can boast up to 1,800 horsepower, reach speeds up to 60 mph, and cover 300 feet in six head-snapping seconds.***

*Bob Chandler Jr. Interview, December, 2004.
**Dan Patrick. Interview, December, 2004.
***Carl Fowler. Interview, December, 2004.

Riding atop his John Deere® tractor, a farmer
prepares to compete in a tractor pull in Minnesota.

the Modified Class, where tractors have as many as five engines, also known as blowers, and blast across farm fields or
fan packed arenas, yanking up to 60,000 pounds on a transfer sled. A **transfer sled** is a type of flat trailer hooked to the
back of the tractor. In the competition, the weight is loaded
on the rear of the sled, but as the tractor gains speed, the load
is moved, or "transferred," to the front of the sled.

Carl now sells and repairs everyday tractors that meet
a wide range of needs for their owners, and competes

10–12 times a year. What he loves to do is modify tractors for the wild and wacky world of competition. Today, he enjoys watching his 18-year-old grandson, Erik Lambert, who has begun to compete.[3]

If you visit Carl in Bennington, Vermont, you'll see a small sign along rural Route 9 that reads "Carl's Tractors." You'll notice traction machines and farm implements on the surrounding fields and on the grounds of his business. More tractors can be seen inside his shop, and upstairs, his office overflows with tractor models and tractor memorabilia. There are all kinds of vehicles in various colors, styles, and brands. Posters, signs, and calendars about rigs are piled alongside dozen of magazines and books devoted to tractors.

Much has changed since the early days of farming, when a group of local "tillers of the soil" would meet at day's end when the plowing was done to compare their horses' power or their tractor engines' pull capability. "Mine's bigger or better than yours," they would wager. Today, tractor pulls are at the smallest country fairs and at Grand National Championship and international competitions, with safety regulations, panels of judges, and television coverage. Thousands sit in the driver's seat and thousands more watch and wonder as man and machine play out the age-old ritual of competing against one another.

It all started with horses and traction engines, and it is still about power and speed and the people who go along for the ride.

2

THE RACES AND
THE RACERS

Monster truck competition and racing began with Bob Chandler and his blue Ford F-250 4 × 4 in St. Louis, Missouri, in 1974. In search of spare parts and fellow enthusiasts for their growing four-wheel-drive vehicle obsession, Bob and his wife Marilyn opened The Midwest Four-Wheel Drive Center. They used their truck to promote their business by trying out new parts and accessories and making it bigger and better to show off to others who had 4 × 4s. Among other things, they added bigger and bigger tires, finally using 66-inch-tall flotation tires made by Firestone, now called Bridgestone/Firestone, Inc. (BFS).

Named *Bigfoot*, Bob's blue pickup grew in size and fame. People loved it because it was big and unusual, and in a short time, the Chandlers had a following of others who were building their own large machines and asking their advice. The monster truck phenomenon was born. These **tricked-out** trucks competed in truck pulls, **mud races**, and off-road competitions that showcased their awesome power and 4WD capabilities, which allows trucks to do tight circles and drive almost sideways.

Thousands of screaming, overjoyed fans watch a *Bigfoot* monster truck ride over a line of cars, flattening them.

In 1981, Bob introduced *Bigfoot* and some friends to car crushing in a Missouri cornfield. He drove his muscle-bound 4 × 4 over two junk cars, climbing over them and crushing them flat. It was a hit in the farm fields at home, and when he tried it a few months later at an event, the fans loved it too. It wasn't long before *Bigfoot* was a star attraction at big pulls and mud-racing events, crushing cars in front of tens of thousands of screaming fans in huge stadiums.

Over the next few years, more than a hundred monster trucks entered the scene and showed up in performance arenas. When event promoters realized these big trucks, which looked like giant dune buggies with fiberglass bodies, were starting to gain serious attention, they scrambled to figure out how to market the growing wave of popularity. Soon, the big-tired monsters were crushing cars, limousines, buses, mobile homes, and other monster trucks. They even popped wheelies in addition to driving over things. There were many contenders, such as the popular *King Kong* driven by Jeff Dane, and *USA #1* driven by Everett Jasmer, but *Bigfoot* remained the king of the monster truck world.

The next development in the monster truck competition took place in 1986 at the Houston Astrodome in an event produced by TNT Motorsports. The event was called monster truck racing. Trucks drove, one at a time, over an obstacle course of hills and groups of junk cars to finish with the best time. This lacked the thrill of side-by-side racing, but within two years, head-to-head competition evolved when TNT Motorsports sponsored the first national championship points series for monster trucks. Because monster truck racing was different from any other motorsport event, no guidelines existed. Races developed that awarded the winners a purse, or prize money, and competitions became part of the point series group of races.

The basic concept for the point series, put forth in 1988, was to hold 40 races in which the muscle-bound trucks would earn points toward a national championship. While a few rules have changed, the competition remains much the same today. Most monster truck competition has been in the form of drag racing though different series can be seen on Speed Channel and Clear Channel as well. The WWE of the monster truck world is more about the drama and show than straight competition. Typically though, vehicles compete in pairs in a series of elimination rounds, which leads to a final round to determine the overall champion. A typical monster truck racing event has from eight to 16 competitors who drive their rigs in a qualifying round to achieve a qualifying time. Based on these times, drivers are paired off so the following races have two competitors each. In each round, one

A set of red, yellow, and green lights called a "Christmas Tree" signals the staging or lining up of vehicles before a race. Here a police officer prepares to race his patrol car against a high school student's '60s vintage Pontiac LeMans in the quarter mile "Beat the Heat" program.

truck is eliminated. The winning truck goes on to compete again until one vehicle is the winner.

At the start of each race, drivers approach the starting line, torque up or rev their engines, and wait for the signal to go. A set of "Christmas Tree" lights, which are red, yellow, and green, flash as signals for the start. This is called **staging**, or lining up the trucks for the start. While waiting for the lights, drivers rev their engines by putting one foot on the gas pedal and holding the truck in place by keeping other foot on the brake pedal. **Red lighting** occurs when a truck moves before the green light goes on. If the truck moves before the green light flashes on, the truck is disqualified from that day of racing. Often, the race is won or lost with the hole shot, which is the driver's ability to torque up and come off the starting line faster than the others.

The straight line courses and oval courses have obstacles. Oval tracks are more challenging because they include turns, more obstacles, and longer driving times. Steep entrance ramps make trucks fly into the air as drivers try to clear the cars below them and land smoothly on the exit ramps. A driver's knowledge of how to keep the truck from rolling over is an important skill needed for monster truck racing. The driver has to maneuver the truck onto the entrance ramp in a way that keeps it straight in the air, then land squarely with all four tires on the exit ramp or the ground. Not taking off correctly or not landing on all four wheels can cause a forward or sideways rollover. This occurs when a truck flips end over end or rolls over on its side. Getting **big air**, when the monster truck is off the ground and in the air, is a crowd-pleasing thrill, but if not done correctly, it can result in a rollover in which the truck breaks up or the driver is injured.

Some monster trucks have clear floors, made of lexan, to aid drivers so they can see the placement of their wheels and the surface below them. Modifications such as this and other modifications to monster truck racing have changed the design of monster trucks, increasing the need for safety standards.

Bob Chandler led the pack in 1988 when he gathered a group of interested parties to discuss forming a safety-oriented organization. Some serious injuries and a few deaths had occurred in the early days of monster truck racing, and Bob wanted to prevent that from happening again. They formed the Monster Truck Racing Association (MTRA) to focus on safety issues for spectators and drivers. Today, monster truck owners, drivers, prompters, and sponsors are members of the MTRA. Many safety rules have developed as a result of mishaps, and as MTRA members and officials evaluate the mishaps, they continue to learn from them.

Grave Digger "pops a wheelie" while crushing a car during the Monster Truck Challenge in New York at the Orange County Fair Speedway.

Safety regulations have become stricter each year as the competitions change and the courses become more difficult. The number of outdoor venues, three-day competitions instead of one-day competitions and freestyle competitions have increased. The competing time is longer with bigger obstacles such as vans, buses, fire trucks, and tractor trailers to crush.

Today, events are promoter-controlled and competitors need to be invited to participate. Many competitors have health insurance and workers compensation through their employers and most tracks require proof of liability insurance. The level of professionalism in the sport has risen with strict regulations about alcohol at events.

Monster truck racing has attracted women as well. In 1985, Marilyn Chandler, Bob's wife and business partner, became the sport's first female driver. She appeared on July 4 at Jack Murphy Stadium, in San Diego, California, in *Ms. Bigfoot*, a Ford Ranger chassis modified to accommodate 48-inch tires and the stresses of a 571-cubic-inch, 1,000-horsepower, supercharged Ford aluminum **Hemi engine**. It was the last Bigfoot vehicle to begin life as a factory production pickup truck. Two years later, *Ms. Bigfoot* was revamped with new artwork and paint and renamed *Bigfoot Ranger*. It then made monster truck history by becoming the only Bigfoot truck to be sold for private, nonperformance use.

Pam Vaters of Maryland, a respected, professional monster truck racer, was once the only woman in the United States certified to compete in national events. To become certified, a driver must have an MTRA Class A driver's license, which is earned by performing a checklist of driving skills and having knowledge of safety skills that another MTRA member checks and approves.

"There's a lot of work to getting a Class A license," Pam explains. "First, you get a Class B license by taking a driving test in a monster truck to show that you're capable of driving it well, doing things like accelerating, braking, and turning. Then you have to drive in ten races, sponsored by three different promotional companies and have a Class A-licensed driver sign for each race to verify that you drove safely and competently. It's hard because you either have to have your own truck or have someone trust you to drive their truck, but it's worth it for everyone because of the safety for the drivers and the spectators."

Pam grew up on her grandparents' farm and describes herself as a tomboy when she was a young girl. "I did everything the boys did from driving tractors to motorcycles," she explains, but she never dreamed she would grow up to become one of the country's most recognized racers or to drive the world's largest racing vehicles.

Pam married Michael Vaters, who started his career in 1982 by traveling around the country to special events and custom car shows with a built-up Ford F-250 street truck named *The Black Stallion*. The truck was set up with 44-inch street tires and a 6-cylinder engine that produced 300 horsepower. In 1984, he started "rounding up parts from around the country" to make his tall truck a monster truck and worked about a year and a half on the transformation. In 1986, he toured the United States with a stunt team known as the Hell Drivers and drove in exhibitions and car-crushing events.

"You name it, we've probably crushed it: watermelons, pizzas, boats, campers, farm equipment," said Tim Hall, of Hall Brothers Racing in of Champaign, Illinois, who has served as the president of MTRA.*

Firestone makes the 66 × 43 × 25 Flotation Tire on *Bigfoot*. The average cost is about $1,800 each. *Bigfoot #5* uses Firestone 120 × 48 × 68 tires.**

*Tim Hall. Interview, December, 2004.
**Ken Broadbeck. Interview, December, 2004.

After several injuries, Michael upgraded *The Black Stallion* with suspension components such as springs and shocks to improve suspension travel and to create a softer, gentler landing for himself and the truck. He decided to design a monster truck using a van body since all the other competitors at that time used pickup trucks. *Boogey Van*, equipped with an alcohol-injected, 572 cubic-inch engine, was born in Michael and Pam's garage.

This is where Pam came into the picture. "Pam used to say that she was going to be the driver of *Boogey Van*, and I thought she was just kidding," Michael says. "But one day, a box showed up, and when I opened it, I pulled out a purple driving suit and saw that the blood type on it was Pam's."

Michael admits that he was nervous at first because of the risk of injury while racing, but he set up the cab for her. When he saw her clear three cars and land on all four wheels during her first jump, he knew Pam was good. In 1995, the pair hired a racing expert to work on the engine. It all paid off. That year, she placed fifth in the country. After putting up with teasing from some of the male drivers at the beginning of her career, she turned heads with her winning performances. "In my first points race, I beat *Bigfoot*, which was a huge accomplishment," describes Pam, "but the best part was that Bob Chandler was happy for me. Another achievement was that I made the *Carolina Crusher* red light one time when we were on the starting line together."

Though Pam's racing career had many happy moments, she had some hard ones, too. Pam once spent four days in an intensive care unit after running into the wall (she took out 14 feet of it) at the Pontiac Silverdome in her truck, but she was back to racing within a month. Today, Pam has hung up her helmet to spend more time with son Michael Jr. on their

Black Smith "gets big air" and delights spectators during the Monster Truck Challenge at the Orange County Fair Speedway in New York.

100-acre farm in Hagerstown, Maryland. It's no surprise that Michael Jr. has his eye on racing monster trucks when he gets older.[4]

Dawn Creten met her husband Jimmy at a concert in Bismark, North Dakota, after a monster truck show. Jimmy was into racing, so she went on the road with him, along with a crew member Jimmy was coaching to race. At the last minute, when the crew member couldn't perform, Jimmy offered Dawn the spot and taught her. When he introduced a second truck in 1998, it became Dawn's. Now, she is a mother of 4-year-old Hope and 5-year-old Faith, and she participates in dozens of shows a year.

Today, Dawn finds competing in monster trucks fun and challenging. "I love people, I love talking with them, and I love the fans," explains the petite racer, who is 5 feet 4 inches and 110 pounds and drives *Scarlet Bandit*. "I get excited to win, but putting on a good show is important, too."[5]

Bob Chandler Jr. and *Bigfoot* have stayed on the cutting edge of monster trucks and competition. Hundreds of monster trucks have come to life as a result of his dad's blue Ford F-250 and the "bigger could be better" theory. Bob and Marilyn's dream became a true American success story that they passed down to their son. It has spawned a sport now known and loved around the world.

3

TRUCKS: FACTS AND FIGURES

To build the average monster truck takes from three months to a year. The main elements that go into changing an everyday pickup or van into a monster truck are the chassis, suspension, and horsepower. The chassis is the frame of a vehicle on which parts, such as the body, engine, transmission, suspension, axles, and wheels, are mounted. It has to be strong to withstand the pounding of car crushing and landing after getting air. Tubular chassis with metal or steel tubes welded together are popular because they are lighter in weight and stronger than the old style frames. They are easier to maintain and repair.

The vehicle's suspension is a mechanical system attached to the chassis and smoothes the ride. It can include some or all of the following: coil springs, leaf springs, shock absorbers, airbags, and cantilevers, which are L-shaped hinged units that move like elbows to give more suspension "travel." This is important because these 10,000-plus-pound giants fly through the air and sometimes land with bone-jarring impact.

What makes them fly is horsepower, the unit of measure of an engine's power. All racing monster trucks can have only

A mother and daughter marvel at a monster truck engine on display at the "Monster Trucks: The Science of Extreme Machines" exhibit at the Museum of Science and Industry in Chicago, Illinois.

one automobile engine no larger than 572 cubic inches. But mechanics can add superchargers, powerful fans that blow fuel and air into the engine to increase power. Your family car likely has about 150 to 250 horsepower. The first monster trucks had 500 to 1,000 horsepower. Modern monster trucks have more than 2,000 horsepower.

The **drivetrain** is the system by which the wheels get power from the engine. It takes special parts in the transmission and drivetrain to use the horsepower in a safe, effective way. Most monster trucks have 4WD systems, in which the engine's power goes to all four wheels. Many monster trucks have **four-wheel steering**, a feature that allows the back wheels to be steered as well as the front wheels.

Other important parts include tires, body panels, and safety features. Most monster trucks use the 66-inch flotation tires made by BFS primarily for use on big farm vehicles. The biggest tires used today are 10-foot-tall **Alaska Tundra tires** first made during WWII for land trains in Alaska. Bob Chandler has used these on two of his Bigfoot trucks. Body panels include the fenders, the cab, bedsides, hood, and tailgate. Many monster trucks use fiberglass body panels, which makes it possible to put different bodies on one chassis. The Bigfoot crew first started experimenting with body panels in 1991 and has created many different looks and names on the tubular chassis of their fleet of trucks.

"The chassis are still tubular, but now they are lighter and trucks have better suspension up to 30 inches of wheel travel," says Dan Patrick. "The chassis used to have 450 feet of tubing, but some have approximately 600 feet, which makes it more durable. The drivers are still protected, but the chassis is less forgiving, so there is less damage in an accident. We want things that tumble."[6]

"There have been no big leaps since '99, but continuous small advances, such as shock technology (now adjusted from the outside, which is a time-saver), plus transmissions are more dependable with a longer lifespan and are more durable to withstand impact," he adds.[7]

Because monster trucks can travel at high speeds, and sometimes roll over, safety features are important. All major event promoters require that monster trucks be inspected and certified by the MTRA, with certain parts of the vehicle checked bi-annually or annually. Trucks have to meet more than 100 safety requirements. All trucks have a roll cage, or a cage made

Nomex® fire suits and head protection are a great improvement in the safety of monster truck drivers' and all race car drivers' safety.

of steel tubes, that goes inside the cab to protect the driver during an accident or rollover. A Radio Ignition Interrupter (RII), standard on monster trucks, allows someone on the sidelines to shut off the engine. The RII has been upgraded so other signals can't interfere and shut the truck off by accident.

Another improvement is the certified, three-layer **Nomex®** fire driver's suits required for competitions. Seat belts must be replaced every two years. Today's helmets are lighter and, therefore, create less impact to the neck in a crash.

"If you have a $5 head, you buy a $5 helmet," says Dan Patrick, who has always been an innovator in safety and has always worn a three-layer Nomex® suit. "The average suit can run from $250 to $2,000, and helmets from $80 to $600. Safety has a price, but the majority of people don't worry about safety until it becomes a hindrance to them. If the truck breaks in half, I want the driver to get out and say, 'Man, that was a good ride.'"[8] For competitor Tim Hall "safety equipment is cheaper than the ambulance ride to the hospital."[9]

Bob Chandler categorized the history of monster trucks into three stages. Stage One refers to the first generation of monster trucks, which were built for car crushing. Stage Two describes the second generation of monster trucks, which had stronger frames to survive the wilder car-crushing performances. They also had bigger engines and were easier to maneuver. Stage Three represents the third generation of monster trucks, the ones we see today. They are being developed with a tubular chassis and a super-absorbing suspension to reduce bouncing and to provide better control and safety. They are lightweight and have powerful engines built for racing.

The first Four-Wheel Jamboree Nationals, considered the country's premier 4 × 4 event, attracted 700 participating vehicles and more than 20,000 spectators for competitions in mud bogging, truck pulling, and **show-n-shine**, a competition for the best-built and most attractive trucks. In 2004, this event grew to 14 Jamborees a year in various locations across the United States. Indianapolis, Indiana, is still the center of the Four-Wheel Jamboree Nationals and attracts thousands of participating vehicles, scores of non-

A Jeep Wrangler trudges through the mud during the Mud Bog Fun Runs at the 10th Annual Bond Auto Parts 4-Wheel Jamboree Nationals in Essex Junction, Vermont.

competing 4 × 4s, and more than 100,000 fans. Today, millions of live spectators see monster trucks each year.

Bigfoot 4 × 4 teams tour the United States and have continual television exposure. *Bigfoot* is the most widely seen and recognized performance vehicle in history. Bigfoot trucks have appeared in countless television shows and movies, including *Cannonball Run 2*, *Police Academy 6*, *Tango and Cash*, and numerous ESPN segments, television series, and specials. The trucks have also appeared in Ford and McDonald's commercials. There are Bigfoot home videos, and the Microsoft Corporation teamed with Bigfoot to produce a CD-ROM game with realistic, detailed simulations of monster truck driving, car crushing, and racing. Today, there are a number of games and videos, simulating different competitors.

Though they no longer race for the team, some notable Bigfoot alumni impress monster truck fans. *Bigfoot 6*, built in 1986 and a record-holder for jumping 13 cars in 1987, was sold to an English promoter and still tours under a different name in Europe. Now an attraction at Race Rock Cafe in Orlando, Florida, the only motor sports theme restaurant in the world, *Bigfoot 7* has ten-foot-tall tires.

Bigfoot trucks use different kinds of fuel. For example, *Bigfoot 5*, which has Alaska Tundra tires, guzzles high-octane racing gas for its events. But *Bigfoot 11* and *Bigfoot 8* use methanol in a specialized Jaz fuel cell.

DID YOU KNOW?

The business has many important names, but important to mention are the Hall brothers (Tim and Mark), who started in the mid-1980s with *Big Boss* and *Heavy Metal*, added the *Executioner*, and now ride *Raminator* and its twin brother, *Rammunition*. Drivers for this team have captured Rookie of the Year, Truck of the Year, and Driver of the Year awards, and Tim Hall was awarded the Mechanic of the Year in 2003.*

Snake Bite was the first "3D," or "character body," monster truck. Created by Bigfoot and Mattel Toys, its fiberglass body was brought to life by GTS Fiberglass of Wentzville, Missouri. *Macho Man* was inspired by Randy "Macho Man" Savage, a professional wrestler. The truck sports one of the world's largest fiberglass cowboy hats and a giant pair of sunglasses.

*Tim Hall. Interview, December, 2004.

A new line of World Wrestling-themed miniature toy trucks was kicked off with this event in New York City. The monster truck *Nitro* rides over two cars resembling New York City taxis.

An offshoot of the Bigfoot phenomenon is Wrestletrucks. The concept grew out of monster truck sumo wrestling, an event in which two monster trucks were hooked together to force each other out of the arena's ring. In 1995, the new concept of Wrestletrucks, designed to create more radical action, was taken one step further, combining real wrestlers with monster trucks to create outrageous new trucks and spectacular new events.

Turner Broadcasting's World Championship Wrestling approached Bigfoot's Hollywood agents, and after several hundred hours, numerous melted truck transmissions, and thousands of dollars, a pair of trucks were developed which were personalized after World Wrestling Champion's icon Hulk Hogan and the "baddest" guy on the circuit, "The Giant." *The Hulkster* and *Dungeon of Doom* were built on the *Bigfoot 9* and *Bigfoot 8* chassis, which were extensively remodeled and can accommodate copilots, or a second set of drivers. Since they race longer than regular monster trucks (about 10 minutes instead of two), they are copiloted by pro wrestlers.

"The industry constantly reinvents itself and right now freestyle competitions are the most popular," says Dawn Creten. "TV is broadcasting more events and the competitions are more focused on destruction, partly because the trucks are so much more agile and more can be done with them. The industry is more legitimate today, it's more of a main stream sport, and the events are better attended."[10]

"Hired drivers are now more prevalent than owner/ operators because the industry is now large enough to have larger teams with more than one truck—multi-truck teams," explains Tim Hall. "There are easily 200 to 300 monster truck owners, and many now do it for a hobby and there are many different series now."[11]

4

TRACTORS: A HISTORY

The first tractors were horse and ox teams. They were used for pulling, but work was limited because the animals could not do more than six hours of heavy labor a day, travel more than 13 to 15 miles, and they could get stuck in the fields. Spring work was the hardest because the fields needed to be prepared and planted, and horses were often out of shape after the winter. In addition, horses and oxen required food, care, and maintenance, whereas mechanical tractors only needed fuel.

Nicholas Joseph Cugnot, a Frenchman, was the first person to travel in a self-propelled vehicle. In 1765, he built a machine powered by a massive steam engine that could travel six miles per hour (mph). It had three wooden wheels and a frame of heavy wooden timbers. He called it a "steam wagon," but because it was designed to pull heavy loads, it was the first tractor. These early developments in Europe came before similar inventions in the United States by close to a century.

Nearly 85 years later, Robert Ransome of England built a "farmer's engine" designed to work in the field and operate machinery. This inventor added a steering component, which was connected to an axle, and the phenomenon was off and running.

Bert Rhodes, the author's grandfather, is pictured here in 1915 driving his work-horses as they pull a sickle-bar mower. Farm helper, Steve Pratt, looks on.

In the United States, Jeremy Increase Case introduced his first steam engine in 1869. It was crude, but it did the job well when compared to horses. It is no surprise, then, that the first steam tractors gained in popularity in the 1870s and were known as horse steering engines. Mostly used for plowing, they were **self-propelled**, but not self-steering, and had "simple" and "compound" engines with one or two cylinders.

Despite their benefits, they had many difficulties, such as boiler explosions, backfiring gas, and fire hazards from the sparks released from the smokestack. A load of hay commonly caught fire, and occasional roadway accidents and human injuries occurred. In addition, these engines startled

Bert Rhodes is shown on one of his steam tractors. This photograph was taken in 1900.

horses unused to the commotion. This led to safety laws, one of which, made in 1899, required that the operator "send a man at least 50 yards ahead to warn teams of drivers," that a steam engine was coming through.

It was Nicholas Otto's gasoline engine, built in 1876 in Germany, that started a flurry of development of the internal combustion engine in Europe and in the United States. Two-wheeled, three-wheeled, and four-wheeled vehicles, as well as gas-powered tractors, resulted. Though gas-powered engines were quickly valued for their efficiency, they had many skeptics. By 1917, gasoline-powered and kerosene-powered tractors were the new design, and during World War I, steam tractors were starting to go the way of ox carts and horse teams.

It was carpenter and blacksmith John Froelich, of Iowa, who developed the first gas-powered tractor in 1892 and a year later started the Waterloo Gasoline Traction Engine Company. He sold two tractors based on his prototype with a single-cylinder, vertical engine that developed 20 horsepower. This inventor developed reverse gearing, allowing the tractors to back up. This Waterloo Gasoline Traction Engine Company tractor had one forward and one reverse gear. The same year, the JI Case Threshing Machine Company, of Racine, Wisconsin, entered the tractor market and developed a large, cross-motor machine. This prototype and the first Case tractor had a two-cylinder horizontal engine that produced 20 horsepower, but ignition and carburetor problems discouraged commercial promotion.

Engineering students C.W. Hart and C.H. Parr of Charles City, Iowa, were the first to use the term "tractor." In 1902, they established the Hart-Parr Company and built a 2-cylinder, 4-stroke engine that produced 30 horsepower. This tractor still ran 17 years later, an unusual feat for that time. The following year, they designed another model with water injection to prevent engine knock. It weighed seven tons and is now on display at the Smithsonian Institution, in Washington, D.C.

In 1907, Henry Ford, best known for his car and truck models, designed his first tractor, made up mostly of car parts. It sported the wheels from a binder, the 4-cylinder petrol engine from a "Model B" car, and the front axle and steering gear from a "Model K" car. This great inventor's first tractor model had a transversely mounted engine, and

Henry Ford, pictured here sitting upon one of his first tractors in 1908, used a car engine from a Model-B to power his revolutionary tractors.

its four individual cylinders produced 20 horsepower. It is on display at the Greenfield Village and Henry Ford Museum in Dearborn, Michigan. In 1915, Ford formed a new corporation, Henry Ford and Son, to design and produce tractors on a commercial scale, and it wasn't long before he was selling them for the farm fields of the United States as well as exporting the well-respected Fordson tractor to Europe and Russia. These tractors were built to allow farmers to make repairs easily and quickly.

The mergers of several companies, including McCormick and Deering, led to the birth of another well-respected tractor-maker, The International Harvester Company. Opening up shop in Chicago, Illinois, in 1902, International Harvester made one of the first tractors designed with a one-piece, cast-metal frame and introduced innovative designs for stronger engines after WWI. In 1924, they began selling the Farmall, which revolutionized the industry at that time.

By 1918, more than 140 companies sold tractors and refined designs to make more efficient and less expensive versions. Many inventors of this period shared concepts and designs with motor car and tractor developers. In 1925, more than 500,000 tractors performed the work of over a million and a half horses and thousands of men. During this boom, many companies began to manufacture tractors, but few of them remain today.

The first tractor wheels were steel with lugs added later for better traction. Differently sized lugs were bolted on for different terrain and conditions. It was a time-consuming operation, however, to attach and detach different lugs or special rims to mud-caked wheels that sometimes worked in farm fields and, at other times, traveled on dirt roads. In the 1920s and 1930s, the Allis-Chalmers Company gained fame for fitting pneumatic, or rubber, tires on a rig. The Model U not only became a trendsetter but also a record-setter, with its low-pressure, inflatable tractor tires.

A sales campaign for this tractor's speed advantage resulted in a series of publicity stunts. Barney Oldfield, who had established a reputation as an internationally recognized race car driver, drove the tractor over a mile-long course in Dallas, Texas, at an average speed of 64.28 mph. The event was officially observed by the American Automobile Association and was documented as a world speed record for agricultural tractors. Popularity spread when Allis-Chalmers hired a team of well-known racing drivers to participate in events at state fairs where modified tractors with the pneumatic tires, made by Firestone, raced at speeds of 30 mph and higher.

Another stunt was set up to attract the attention of farmers who attended the International Livestock Exposition in Chicago, Illinois, in 1933. A Model U was driven from Milwaukee, Wisconsin, to Chicago on the highway, a distance of 88 miles, in five hours and one minute. It was said that some Allis-Chalmers dealers, seeking attention, purposely drove their tractors on public roads at speeds calculated to get convictions for traveling too fast. In the end, Allis-Chalmers and low-pressure inflatable tires were a success. In 1934, the Model U was replaced by the WC Tractor, designed specifically for the new tires and priced at $825. A **steel-wheeled** version sold for $150 less.

During World War II, rubber was rationed, and many tractors again rode on steel wheels. But by the late 1940s, the technology that increased speed and efficiency ruled the land, and soon all tires were made from rubber.

During the first and second World Wars, some tractors were cloaked with sheet metal and put into service as tanks and multipurpose vehicles. The Killen-Strait military prototype, built in 1915, is considered the first **track-laying armored vehicle**. Made in the United States, the tractor was sent to Great Britain, where it was produced as a tank and fitted with the body shell of a Delaunay-Belleville armored car.

The Daimler Horse, built in 1915 by auto and engine developer Gottlieb Daimler to replace horses for moving war equipment, was a two-wheeled traction unit with a 4-cylinder engine that produced 14.5 horsepower. Following the war, it was revamped for farm work and led to the Pugh motor plow,

C.L. Best Tractor Company invented this 75 hp Tracklayer tractor. However, the first, track-laying armored vehicle is believed to have been the Killen-Strait military prototype in 1915.

which eventually spawned the Austrian Steyr-Daimler-Puch tractor range.

The next major developments in ideas and inventions following the wars added comfort and convenience features. At first, they were options, but they soon became standard. During the 1940s and 1950s, tractor makers such as the Minneapolis-Moline Company began building tractors with cabs to protect farmers from the weather and offered models with air conditioning, heating, and a radio. Cabbed models like the Minneapolis-Moline U-DLX brought tractors up to the level of cars by offering a fold-up passenger-side seat and gearing that allowed everyday travel of up to 40 mph. The fifth gear was a road gear that made it possible for a farmer and his family to drive into town on a Saturday night or attend church on Sunday morning. Sheet metal, along with a stylized grille, bumper, headlamps, and a cab with flip-out front and side windows, made the tractor look like a road car.

The John Deere Company, started by blacksmith and engine-plow developer John Deere at the turn of the century and carried forward by family members, moved tractor development light years ahead in the 1950s and 1960s with the development of special purpose-built tractors and tractors with multicylinder engines, power brakes, and power steering. Deere developed an attractive new green and yellow paint scheme and advertised "Power to meet every need . . . six power sizes . . . 30 basic models."

On August 29, 1960, thousands came to the Cotton Bowl in Dallas, Texas, for an exhibition of John Deere's new four-

Because tractor inventions paralleled and interfaced with automobile development, many name plates on tractors were familiar in the car world. The "Big Three" auto makers in the United States today—General Motors, Ford, and Chrysler (now DaimlerChrysler)—all produced tractors, engines, or tractor parts. Ford was the most influential by far, along with inventors and carmakers like Mercedes-Benz, Fiat, and Renault.

cylinder engines. Mounted inside a new lineup of tractors labeled the 1010, 2010, 3010, and 4010 Series, Deere's new generation of power produced 36 to 84 horsepower, and over the next decade the company went on to sell over 400,000 of these tractors.

Though made earlier, 4WD versions of tractors became more popular and were followed by tractors with increased horsepower and improved performance. In 1978, a typical "monster tractor" had 747 hp and weighed 95,000 pounds when empty.

The tractor industry today is global. Tractors are used throughout the world, and parts for tractors are produced around the world. Over the years, since the days of early tractor development, many companies have bought out others to form larger companies and share technology. In the United States today, the major tractor manufacturers are AGCO, John Deere, and New Holland-Case.

5

TRACTORS: FACTS AND FIGURES

Today, there are many different types of tractors. Some examples are the row crop tractor with wheels that adjust in and out for crops that grow in rows; the standard tractor, often used in wheat fields, with wheels that do not adjust; high crop tractors, taller versions used for cultivating and spraying higher crops; and orchard tractors that have pointed fenders that slide over the wheels so as not to damage the fruit, blossoms, or branches of orchard crops. An articulated tractor is a large tractor with parts that turn as well as the wheels. A chicken tractor is not a real tractor, but a chicken coop on wheels that is pulled around to spread fertilizer.

Tractors have large and small wheels, with different tread designs on their tires. Some wheel-design types are single-wheel tractors, which have one front wheel. A tricycle tractor has two wheels close together, and the wide front-end tractor has two wheels that are spread apart. Larger tractors can have from two or four tires on each side. Tractor wheels are smaller in the front than in back. Rear wheels provide the most traction and support and, therefore, need to have the greatest amount of ground contact. Smaller front tires make steering easier and allow a smaller turning radius.

Antique tractors, like this red one, have two-toed front wheels that make tight turns and steering easier over bumpy terrain.

Tread patterns will continue to evolve in the future and as the equipment becomes larger, even bigger tires or tires designed to carry heavier loads will be necessary. "Tires now have better tread designs because the faster speeds require a better tread," says Ken Broadbeck, an engineer for BFS, which is the leading manufacturer of tires in the United States. "They are also tougher, more resistant to the wear and tear of the field. New is a 'severe service' tire for 4WD tractors used in construction." In the future, the speed will continue to increase, so tire technology will have to keep up with that. Tractors can now go 30 mph; 20 years ago, they could only go 20 mph, and there are tractors in England that can exceed 40 mph."

Over time, 4WD tractors, with power delivered to the front and rear wheels, have become popular. 4WD tractors can do more work, so smaller tractors can do the job of big-

Rubber-tracked tractors, like this one, have become more popular over the past 15 years because they are excellent for farming wet terrain.

ger tractors. Most farming tractors start in the category of engines that produce 350 to 400 horsepower. The majority are farm-oriented, but some of these tractors are used for industrial purposes. Caterpillar makes the "Challenger" series of crawler, or **rubber-tracked**, tractors that have become popular, especially in farm fields in the west. A rubber track spreads out the weight of the tractor so soil is compacted less. Compact tractors, with 15 to 17 horsepower, are becoming popular and are used as all-purpose tractors by homeowners. Many come from Asia.

Back in the days of John Deere and his Poppin' John's, tractor engines were small and had only two cylinders. By the 1960s, the need for increased power and speed led

The interior of a modern tractor affords this farmer a panoramic view and offers protection from the elements.

to the development of three-cylinder, four-cylinder, and six-cylinder engines. A few eight-cylinder engines work on the toughest soil and largest farms. The first tractors were two-speed with forward gears only. Today's tractors have up to 32 forward gears and four to six gears in reverse.

When people buy a tractor today, they are primarily buying the power to perform work. Other objectives, such as fuel efficiency, sound level, dealer price, and service, are important as well. Today's tractors have air conditioners, heaters, radios, and cup holders for coffee or soda cans. Some have closed-circuit televisions so drivers can see the surrounding land.

Jerome Demko, of Lowville, New York, has been driving tractors on his family farm since he was 7 years old. Now 32, Jerome says "there are now standard transmissions, onboard automatic computers, GPS, and tractors that even steer themselves, and there are prototypes for driverless tractors. New advances in technology include different style gears, computers checking drivelines and lighter tractors, titanium and carbon-fiber parts."[12]

All of today's tractors run on diesel fuel. After steam tractors became obsolete, a number of other low-cost fuels such as kerosene, distillate, and gasoline were used. Some tractors in the 1950s and 1960s used propane, and others ran on liquid propane gas. The advantage of diesel fuel is that it develops more of a lugging, or pulling, horsepower and a longer powerstroke. This means that the fuel burns more slowly and helps the engine produce torque, which is the engine's ability to do work. New developments being researched are with hybrid systems and alcohol fuel.

How does a tractor pull its load? Early tractors used a system of belts and pulleys added to the tractor for attaching loads or tools. Next came the draw bar, a simple, straight bar pulled behind the tractor to which equipment was attached. The three-point hitch, a triangular-shaped hitching unit, was developed by Harry Ferguson, and today, a power take-off (PTO) is the standard method of pulling. The PTO is a shaft off the back of the tractor that operates like a driveshaft to run farming implements. A live PTO allows one power source for the tractor and a separate power source for the implements behind it. This means that the tractor can be stopped while power still operates at the rear, such as when baling hay.

All tractors must be tested before they are sold to consumers. Information about tractors built all over the world comes from the University of Nebraska's Nebraska Tractor Test Law (Nebraska Test). All specifications, data, and comparative performance results on tractors are evaluated and fuels are compared. Because over 25,000 injuries and more than 100 deaths occur each year in tractor accidents, the standards are becoming increasingly strict with regard to safety features. In the late 1960s, rollover protection was developed and is now required on all tractors to protect drivers in the event of a rollover. In the past, when a tractor rolled over onto its top or side, there was no protection for the driver. Today, a reinforced structure protects the driver and prevents the cab from collapsing.

The collecting of antique tractors has skyrocketed in popularity, and collectors can be found all over the world. Many people still run tractors that are 50 years old or more, and many of these vehicles can still do a full day's work.

Though farmers have always compared tractors to see whose was the best at pulling, it wasn't until the 1950s that tractor pulls grew from a pastime into a sport. Today, tractor pulls are all over the United States and the world. In Europe, tractor pulling has become popular. These competitions, where tractors pull different amounts of weight, have different classes and include the following: antique, or pre-1960 tractors; out of the field, or modern stock farm tractors; prostock, with one turbocharger to enhance engine performance; superstock, which allows up to four turbochargers; and modified, for tractors with up to five engines and turbochargers or superchargers. Some of these engines are turbine jet or helicopter engines and range in horsepower from 120 to 1,800 with a goal of producing torque and speed. Weights pulled range from 22,000 pounds pulled on a stone boat or wooden boat to up to 60,000 pounds pulled on a transfer

The popularity of tractor pull competitions has grown considerably since its introduction as a sport in the 1950s. Competitions exist for tractors that vary in size, class, and weight.

sled. Today, the competitive tractor governing body is the National Tractor Puller's Association. There is now a new class called Unlimited.

Garner Stone, the owner of G. Stone Motors in Middlebury, Vermont, pulls a modified tractor with a V-12 Allison air engine, and has competed on the Grand National circuit for tractor pulling. His fans consider him to be the Dale Earnhardt Sr. of Tractor Pulling. "You can never have too much horsepower," says Gardner. "It's like having a girl that's too pretty, it just doesn't happen. Tractors are getting bigger and better, and have stronger engines and improved durability."[13]

Men aren't the only fans or participants at tractor pulls. Women also enjoy the sport, as this competitor in an antique tractor pull in Oklahoma demonstrates.

Safety requirements have increased for tractor-pulling competitions and include seat belts, fire suits, and helmets for drivers along with roll bars, which are becoming standard. Explosion blankets protect drivers and fans in the event that parts of the engine fly off the tractor from a malfunction or explosion, and shut-off switches are operated by the tractor driver and the transfer sled driver in the event of an emergency.

Though tractor competition draws mostly men, women also compete and race. In addition to tractor pulls, there are national and international plowing contests, and competitors often have their tractors and plows flown around the world to compete in events. Purses, or cash prizes, are offered at the highest levels of tractor competition. New safety requirements for pulling include a standard roll cage, helmets, and fire suits. The big tractor pulls are getting bigger as the sport expands, with 23 this year versus 15 last year.[14]

No prizes are offered in the antique class of tractor pulling, but the superstock and modified competitions boast purses for winners with the most points. Points are often gathered over the course of a year. For many, however, just as in the early days when farmers gathered in their fields to see whose horse or tractor was the best at the end of the day, the true reward is the fun of competing.

Where it all goes from here is anyone's guess. The history of engines, the evolution of tractors, and the history of *Bigfoot* and the monster trucks have all followed a similar

DID YOU KNOW?

Horsepower is one of the most important but confusing words people encounter when buying a tractor. Horsepower measures the power an engine produces, and the term comes from the days when work was accomplished by the power of a horse.

Tractor competition is a major motorsport, with more than 1,000 members, and is active 10 countries throughout Europe and Australia. In 2004, there were some 250 pulling sessions in the United States and Canada. Some (tractor) competitors are *Sassy Massy, Just Blowin' Smoke, Yes, Deere, Technical Difficulties, Dirt Track Cadillac,* and *Poison Ivy.**

*NTPA materials, *Tractor Puller*, December 2004.

path, starting from the spark of invention and evolving into the spirit of challenge.

Henry Ford would be proud. Or would he? What do you think he would say about cupholders in a tractor or a computer that controls the steering? What do you think he would say about monster trucks and their competitions? Perhaps he would enjoy the spectacle of engines and machinery pushed to their limits as hundreds of thousands of fans of monster trucks and tractors do today.

NOTES

Chapter 1

1. Bob Chandler Jr., Interview, December 2004.

2. Dan Patrick, Interview, December 2004.

3. Carl Fowler, Interview, December 2004.

Chapter 2

4. Pam Vaters, Interview, December 2004.

5. Dawn Creten, Interview, December 2004.

Chapter 3

6. Tim Hall, Interview, December 2004.

7. Dan Patrick, Interview, December 2004.

8. Ibid.

9. Tim Hall, Interview, December 2004.

10. Dawn Creten, Interview, December 2004.

11. Tim Hall, Interview, December 2004.

Chapter 5

12.   Jerome Demko, Interview, December 2004.

13.   Gardner Stone, Interview, December 2004.

14.   Ibid.

CHRONOLOGY

Monster Trucks

1974 Bob and Marilyn Chandler promote their new business, Midwest Four Wheel Drive Center, with their big blue Ford F-250 4 × 4 pickup.

1978 *Bigfoot* becomes the first monster truck to use rear steering.

1979 *Bigfoot* makes its first paid appearance in a car show in Denver, Colorado, and in the movie *Take This Job and Shove It*.

1981 *Bigfoot 2* is built, the first to use 66-inch tires. *Bigfoot's* first car crush for an audience is a huge success.

1983 The first Bigfoot toy is sold by Playskool and becomes the all-time best-selling toy truck. *Bigfoot 3* is built.

1984 *Bigfoot 4* is built and other monster trucks hit the scene in growing numbers. *USA #1* and *King Kong* are two favorites.

1985 *Bigfoot 4* stars in the largest monster truck event in history. 120,000 people attend the two-day event at Anaheim Stadium in California. Marilyn Chandler becomes the first female monster truck driver at the wheel of *Ms. Bigfoot*.

1986 *Bigfoot 5* is built with dual 10-foot (3-meter) Firestone tires, it is the world's tallest, widest, and heaviest pickup truck. The first event is held where monster trucks compete for time over an obstacle course, racing one truck at a time.

1987 *Bigfoot 6* sets a long distance car-jumping record by clearing 13 cars.

1988 *Bigfoot 7* is built for the movie *Roadhouse.*

Side-by-side, or head-to-head, monster truck racing with purse money and points series developed. Bob Chandler initiates the formation of the Monster Truck Racing Association (MTRA), the safety and sanctioning body for this motorsport.

1989 *Bigfoot 8*, the first tubular-chassis race truck, is designed, built, and tested. *Bigfoot 2* becomes the first American monster truck to tour Australia.

1990 *Bigfoot 8* wins 24 of 40 races to capture monster truck racing's National Championship. *Bigfoot 3* appears in Japan at the Tokyo Dome.

1991 Mattel Toys unveils its Bigfoot Champions toy line which sells out immediately.

1992 Bob Chandler introduces the team concept to monster truck racing. *Bigfoot 10* wins national championship by a record margin; *Bigfoot 2* is reborn as *Safarifoot.*

1993 *Bigfoot 3* is reborn as *Safarifoot 2*. *Bigfoot 11*, known as *Wildfoot*, wins the Bigfoot team's third championship.

1994 Dan Patrick's *Samson* is the first monster truck to break the five-second barrier with a run of 4.983 seconds at Bloomsburg, Pennsylvania.

1995 Pam Vaters, first female in the United States certified to compete in national events, places fifth in the nation driving *Boogey Van*.

Wrestletrucks designed to create more radical action by combining wrestlers with monster trucks.

1996 Dan Patrick awarded the first-ever Wreck of the Year Award by MTRA, resulting from the infamous rollover at Bloomsburg, Pennsylvania. Patrick was also awarded the Sportsman Award.

1997 Dan Patrick awarded patent from the U.S. Patent and Trademark Office in Washington, DC, for the first 3-D body design of the *Samson* monster truck.

1998 Over 10 million spectators witnessed some form of live monster truck racing action.

2000 More females are driving, and more families are watching. Television coverage increases, and more events are added. Enthusiasts can buy video games, drive Monster go-karts, and have Monster truck-themed birthday parties.

Tractors

1765 Nicholas Joseph Cugnot, of France, develops first tractor, called a "steam wagon," used to transport soldiers and equipment during wartime.

1849 "Farmer's engine" built by Robert Ransome, in England, had a steering component added to a crude machine design.

1850s Steam power becomes popular in the United States.

1869 First steam engine for farm use introduced in the United States by Jeremy Increase Case.

1870s Horse steering steam engines first used.

1890s Tradition and technology begin to clash, with accidents and incidents between horse teams and new steam engines on farms.

1892 First successful gas-powered engine built by John Froelich of Iowa.

1893 Waterloo Gasoline Traction Engine Company established (later bought by John Deere).

1897 Flour City one-cylinder tractor introduced.

1902 Hart-Parr Company produces a two-cylinder tractor engine; still in use 17 years later.

1906 International Harvester enters the scene.

1918 More than 140 companies are selling tractors in the United States. Tractors replace 1,500,000 horses and 250,000 workers on farms.

1925 More than 50,000 tractors at work on farms.

1933 Pneumatic tires are introduced and become an industry standard by the 1940s.

1950s Manufacturers continue to increase horsepower, include safety features, and begin to emphasize comfort by adding cabs, heaters, and air conditioners.

1960s John Deere introduces multicylinder engines and tractors with power brakes and steering.

1970s Increased horsepower, safety, and standard four-wheel-drive (4WD) feature are emphasized by all makers.

1978 "Monster tractor" trend is in full swing. The typical size is around 95,000 pounds, with a typical strength of about 747 horsepower.

1980s Tractor sales plummet because of tough times for farmers and high fuel prices.

1990s Current trend is toward compact tractors for homeowners, i.e., multipurpose tractors with low horsepower.

2000s More amenities are added to tractors, with radios and televisions, and GPS. Computerization increases, with some driverless tractors and new programs to cultivate and plow rows.

STATISTICS

Information about the National Tractor Pulling Association (NTPA).

What is it?   Farm tractors have now become superstocks. They have added turbochargers and inter-coolers. Now, it's "pull on Sunday, plow on Monday."

Is it safe?   Safety concerns have led to barriers for facilities, and there is greater distance between fans and the track.

Who pulls?   Most are men who prefer motorsports to stick and ball sports, and most are employed in the agricultural and automotive and trucking industries.

NTPA Quick Facts and Stats:

350 event circuit/approximately 1.4 million spectators.
83 percent male, average age 31 years.
78 percent between the ages of 25 and 54.
58 percent earn between $35,000 and $50,000.
78 percent married.
73 percent own a pickup.
84 percent employed in blue collar professions.
80 percent camp, hunt, fish, and boat.
82 percent purchase parts and supplies to maintain their vehicles.

GLOSSARY

4 × 4:   *See* Four-wheel-drive.

Alaska Tundra tires: This is a general term to mean large diameter tires used on vehicles or buggies that motor on the soft tundra of Alaska.

Alcan Highway: Also known as the Alaska-Canada Highway, "The Road," or the Alaska Highway, this 1,522-mile military supply route was built through the wilderness in 1942. It connects Dawson Creek, British Columbia, with Fairbanks, Alaska.

Antique Class: This term refers to classic tractors built before 1960 that pull loads of up to 32,000 pounds on a stone or wooden boat.

Big air: This term is used to mean getting your Monster Truck (or any other vehicle) up in the air.

Drivetrain: These are the components of a vehicle that transmit power and includes axle shafts, drive shafts, universal joints, wheels, tires, manual clutch, and gearbox or automatic transmission.

Four-wheel-drive (4WD):   A system in which the front and rear wheels are connected through a drive shaft and the axles to the transmission, usually through a transfer case. These are often used to mean the same thing and can be used interchangeably. A full-time system is always engaged. A part-time system means your vehicle is in 2WD until you activate it by lever, push button, or some other electromechanical means.

Four-wheel steering: A system in which the front and rear wheels have their own steering linkages.

Hemi engine: A dome-shaped combustion chamber used in racing or high-performance engines.

Inter-cooler: A small heat exchanger, similar to the radiator, used in the engine's cooling system that helps reduce the temperature of air delivered to the engine.

Modified Class: This class includes tractors that have as many as five engines or blowers and blast across farm fields or fan packed arenas, yanking up to 60,000 pounds on a transfer sled.

Mud bogging or mud-racing: This event occurs in deep mud to see how far or how fast a vehicle or tractor can go.

Nomex®:   A flame-resistant material used for all the apparel worn in automotive competition.

Red lighting: This occurs when a truck moves before the green light goes on. If the truck moves before the green light flashes on, the truck is disqualified from that day of racing. Often, the race is won or lost with the hole shot, which is the driver's ability to torque up and come off the starting line faster than the others.

Rubber-tracked: A rubber track spreads out the weight of the tractor thereby reducing the compacting of the soil.

Self-propelled: Nicholas Joseph Cugnot, a Frenchman, was the first person to travel in a self-propelled vehicle. In 1765, he built a machine powered by a massive steam engine that could travel six miles per hour. It had three wooden wheels and a frame of heavy wooden timbers. He called it a "steam wagon," but because it was designed to pull heavy loads, it was the first tractor.

Show-n-shine: This is a form of competition that rewards the best built or most attractive trucks or vehicles.

Staging: At the start of each Monster Truck race, drivers approach the starting line, rev up their engines, and wait for the signal to go. A set of "Christmas Tree" lights, which go from red, yellow, to green, flash as signals for the start. This is called staging, or lining up the trucks for the start of the competition.

Steel-wheeled: These tractors had steel wheels without rubber and sold for less.

Track-laying armored vehicle: The Killen-Strait military prototype, built in 1915, is considered the first track-laying armored vehicle. Made in America, the tractor was sent to Great Britain, where it was produced as a tank and fitted with the body shell of a Delaunay-Belleville armored car.

Transfer sled: A transfer sled is a type of flat trailer hooked to the back of the tractor. When the competition begins, the weight is loaded on the rear of the sled. As the tractor gains speed, the load is moved, or transferred, to the front of the sled.

Tricked-out: This term describes a Monster Truck or other vehicle set up with parts that are bigger and/or better than what it came with from the factory. Often, this means bigger engines, transmissions, wheels, and tires, and other add-ons.

FURTHER READING

Monster Trucks

Brubaker, Ken, and Moor, Tom. *Monster Trucks*. St. Paul, MN: Motorbooks International, 2003.

Hintz, Martin & Kate. *Monster Truck Drag Racing*. Bloomington, MN: Capstone Press, 1996.

Johnston, Scott D. *Monster Truck Racing*. Danbury, CT: Scholastic Library Publishing, 1994.

Johnston, Scott D. *Monster Trucks: The World's Best Monster Trucks in 500 Great Photos*. St. Paul, MN: Motorbooks International, 2005.

Johnstone, Michael. *Monster Trucks*. Minneapolis, MN: Lerner Publications, 2001.

Levete, Sarah. *Monster Trucks*. Orlando, FL: Raintree, 2005.

Nelson, Kristin L. *Monster Trucks*. Minneapolis, MN: Carolrhoda Books, Inc., 2003.

Tractors

Bingham, Caroline. *Tractor*. New York, NY: Dorling Kindersley Publishing, 2004.

Leffingwell, Randy. *The American Farm Tractor: A History of the Classic Tractor*. Osceola, WI: Motorbooks International, 1991.

Johnston, Scott D. *The Original Monster Truck: Bigfoot.* Minneapolis, MN: Capstone Press, 1994.

McKinley, Marvin. *Wheels of Farm Progress.* St. Joseph, MI: The American Society of Agricultural Engineers, 1980.

Miller, Ray H. *Fun Facts About Farm Equipment.* Dyersville, IA: The Ertl Company, Inc., 1995.

Morland, Andrew. *Thoro'bred Tractors.* London: Osprey Publishing, 1990.

Morland, Andrew, and Pripps, Robert N. *The Big Book of Farm Tractors: The Complete History of the Tractor 1855 to Present.* Stillwater, MN: Voyageur Press, 2001.

Murphy, Jim. *Tractors: From Yesterday's Steam Wagons to Today's Turbocharged Giants.* New York, NY: J.B. Lippincott, 1984.

BIBLIOGRAPHY

Broadbeck, Ken. Interview, December 2004.

Chandler Jr., Bob. Interview, December 2004.

Cretin, Dawn. Interview, December 2004.

Demko, Jerome. Interview, December 2004.

Fowler, Carl. Interview, December 2004.

Hall, Tim. Interview, December 2004.

Patrick, Dan. Interview, December 2004.

Stone, Gardner. Interview, December 2004.

ADDRESSES

American Tractor Pullers Association
P.O. Box 39
Charlestown, IN 47111
(812) 752-0800

BIGFOOT 4 × 4 Incorporated
6311 N. Lindbergh Boulevard
St. Louis, MO 63042
(314) 731-2822
bigfoot@bigfoot4x4.com

Early Day Gas Engine & Tractor Association
1537 Weekend Villa Road
Ramona, CA 92065
(760) 789-3402

Manson, Brian
2Xtreme Racing
15812 214th Street
Tonganoxie, KS 66086
(913) 845-8781 Phone
(913) 845-4242 Fax

Monster Truck Racing Association (MTRA)
14843 April Drive
Loxahatchee, FL 33470
(561) 383-7290

The Nashville Network (TNN)
2806 Opryland Dr.
Nashville, TN 37214

National Tractor Puller Association (NTPA)
6155-B Huntley Road
Columbus, OH 43229
(614) 436-1761

PACE Motor Sports
495 N. Commons Drive
Suite 200
Aurora, IL 60504-8187
(630) 566-6100 Phone
(630) 566-6180 Fax

INTERNET SITES

Monster Trucks

www.monstertrucks.net

> *A site dedicated to monster trucks that includes a list of events, television schedule, and a web directory listing other sites related to trucks and the sport.*

www.monstertruckracing.com

> *With over 475 pictures, this site serves as a visual reference for the sport and provides background information on the teams and drivers involved.*

www.monsternationals.com

> *A site showcasing the Monster Nationals, a family-oriented monster truck show with events across the country.*

www.monstermania.com

> *A general monster truck fan site, including event reviews, a photo gallery, wallpaper gallery, special crash mania gallery, and message board.*

www.bigfoot4x4.com

> *The Internet home of Bigfoot, the original monster truck, providing news, an events schedule, a photo gallery, and facts and history related to Bigfoot.*

Tractors

www.ntpapull.com

> The official site of the National Tractor Pullers
> Association (NTPA), including a schedule of events
> and results, current point standings, television
> coverage, and news.

www.atpapullersonline.com

> Representing the American Tractor Pullers
> Association, the site includes event schedules and
> results, television coverage, driver profiles, point
> standings, sponsor information, news, and a
> merchandise store.

www.antiquetractors.com

> A resource site for antique tractors built before
> 1970, including classifieds, a photo gallery, discus-
> sion forums, and a section devoted to garden tractor
> enthusiasm.

www.mytscstore.com/default.asp

> Tractor Supply Company's homepage offering
> all the essentials for home, vehicle, and lawn
> improvement.

http://science.howstuffworks.com/inside-tractor.htm

> An overview of how a competition tractor is put
> together.

INDEX

ABOUT THE AUTHOR

Sue Mead began her automotive career as a part-time freelance evaluator for *Four Wheeler Magazine* in 1988, on the first team that included women as test drivers. Today, she travels the globe test-driving cars and trucks and working as a photo journalist/feature writer for over four dozen publications. Mead specializes in 4WD and has been an auto editor and 4WD editor for CNN/fn. Over the last 18 years, she has accumulated enough off-road miles to have circumnavigated the world in the dirt.

Mead has been a participating journalist on three Camel Trophy adventures in Borneo, Mongolia and Central America. She has been an attending journalist on the following events: the Camel Trophy '98, in Tierra del Fuego, Argentina; for the Land Rover's G4 Challenge, in Australia, in 2003; and for the LONGITUDE team from Singapore to Bangkok, in 2004. She has participated on three record-setting adventure drives: the Arctic Circle Challenge '95, the Tip to Tip Challenge '96, and the TransAmerica Challenge '97. She assisted Mark A. Smith and Jeep Jamboree U.S.A. as the coordinator of the Alaska Jeep Jamborees, in 1996, and 1997.

Mead's off-road racing includes participating in Baja 1000 six times: She was the co-driver for Rod Hall in the 1996 Baja 1000(1st place finish), was the co-driver for Darren Skilton for the 1999 Baja 1000 (1st place finish), was the co-driver in the Baja 2000 on the internationally ranked Mitsubishi team (1st place finish), was the co-driver on the Scaroni Motorsports Team, 2001, and was the driver for two Wide Open Baja/Centrix Teams in the 2002 and 2003

Baja 1000. She was a driver and co-driver for the Primm 300 (1st place) with Darren Skilton. She was the co-driver in the 2000 Paris-Dakar Rally, completed the Nevada 1000, and is featured in the off-road documentary, *Into the Dust*, as a member of the Toyota Motorsports Team, 2002.

Mead writes for *Four Wheeler*, *Four Wheel & Off Road*, *4WD and Sport Utility*, *Off Road*, *Motor Trend*, *Truck Trend*, *Auto Week*, *Popular Science*, *Popular Mechanics*, *Men's Journal*, *Parade*, *The New York Times*, *Road and Track Buyers Guide*, *European Car*, as well as magazines and newspapers around the globe. She is also a correspondent for Motor Trend Radio and has received two awards from the International Automotive Press Association.

Mead has written *Monster Trucks and Tractors*. New York, NY: Chelsea House Publishers, 1998.

ACKNOWLEDGEMENTS

Special thanks to Brooke Mead and Ted Grozier, who helped with the research and editing of this book and to Tara McKay and Ginny Wehner, who helped with the typing.

Other thanks to Robert A. George, Carl Fowler, Bob Chandler and Bob Chandler Jr., Pam and Michael Vaters, Dawn and Jimmie Creten, Dan Patrick, Jim Galusha, Jerome Demko, Tara Mello, Meghan Searles, Garner Stone, and Ginny Wehner.

Photo Credits:

© AP/Wide World Photos: Cover, 18, 27, 29, 31, 47; © AFP/ Getty Images: 33; © Bettmann/CORBIS: 39; © Duomo/ CORBIS: 7, 9, 16; © DUOMO/Duomo/CORBIS: 20, 24; © Joe Bator/CORBIS: 48; © Michael S. Yamashita/CORBIS: 51; © Phil Schermeister/CORBIS: 13; © Tim Wright/CORBIS: 46; © Getty Images: 11, 42, 52; © Sue Mead: 36, 37.

Nomex® is a registered trademark of E. I. duPont de Nemours and Company.